YOUR KNOWLEDGE HAS VALUE

Bibliographic information published by the German National Library:

The German National Library lists this publication in the National Bibliography; detailed bibliographic data are available on the Internet at http://dnb.dnb.de .

Imprint:

Copyright © 2012 GRIN Verlag, Open Publishing GmbH
Print and binding: Books on Demand GmbH, Norderstedt Germany
ISBN: 978-3-668-12610-7

This book at GRIN:

http://www.grin.com/en/e-book/313521/why-beauty-matters-the-transformational-experiences-of-art-and-music-upon

Cyrus Manasseh, Pamela Schmidt

Why Beauty Matters. The Transformational Experiences of Art and Music upon the Human Soul

GRIN Publishing

GRIN - Your knowledge has value

Since its foundation in 1998, GRIN has specialized in publishing academic texts by students, college teachers and other academics as e-book and printed book. The website www.grin.com is an ideal platform for presenting term papers, final papers, scientific essays, dissertations and specialist books.

Visit us on the internet:

http://www.grin.com/

http://www.facebook.com/grincom

http://www.twitter.com/grin_com

Why Beauty Matters:
The Transformational Experiences of Art and Music upon the Human Soul

PROFESSIONAL ESSAY.
A JOINT RESEARCH ESSAY AUTHORED IN 2012
BY **Cyrus Manasseh, Pamela Schmidt**

We recognize the great exultation with the life of great artists like Beethoven and we realize that all artists praise and exult life. (Agnes Martin and Dieter Schwartz 1992)

We can define beauty as a combination of qualities such as shape, color, form, or sound that satisfies aesthetic appreciation within us; these can be said to be the aggregate qualities of an experience that give pleasure to the senses or pleasurably exalts the mind and spirit.

Art and music affect our consciousness by giving us experiences that can challenge the viewer through emotional, spiritual, ethical, intuitive, and psychological processes. Their transformative power is based on the view that beauty does not reside in any object but within the experience, one has with it. The brain's circuits flooding with neurochemicals which create heightened euphoric feelings simultaneously intensify these feelings. Through this, beauty awakens us and has the ability to create positivity and transcendent experiences.

Beauty originates from our intuition and feelings. We often feel and sense beauty more than we can see it. When we are in the presence of beauty, we subjectively inhabit a sacred space of creation. We hear it in the sounds of nature, in the sounds of waves crashing on a beach and when we look up in a night sky with stars. Our senses respond to this immersion of light, color, and sound which enchant the eye and ear. As such, the immediacy and visibility of beauty can astound us. Through our pleasure in perceiving it, we come to rest, are silenced, and are placed in awe by its qualitative and structural features. When beauty opens our hearts it releases in us our ability to care for what is just and true. The triumvirate of western values—truth, beauty, and goodness—have long served as the foundation for positive human development and for many of us, our experience of beauty takes us deep within ourselves to the most intimate sense of who we are and what we have endured. In its various forms and manifestations, beauty has profound neurological and psychological impact and is the ultimate attractor and healer that helps us to transcend negativity. It is restorative and inspires us to heal, repair, and move forward.

From the beginning of civilization, musicians and artists have created dynamic work inviting us into a divine realm and transcendental world. Beauty has a spiritual foundation and the capacity to create connectedness.

As a baby regards a mother's face, this first acknowledgement, combines familiarity, bonding, and beauty. The baby's concentration increases the positive connection. This connectedness lies all around us and in fact, is palpable in everyday life. We experience it in our contemplation of what is pleasingly familiar and in the ability to see the sacred in the world. Yet often to see beauty, and be inspired by this experience, we need to make time, decrease the distractions, and allow this to occur. The practice of meditation can facilitate a slowing down of our thoughts and provide a way to regard the world from a calmer perspective so that beauty can be seen.

The immersion into beauty has the power to stimulate optimal experiences described as "flow states". According to Mihaly Csikszentmihalyi, flow is being able to reach a state of effortless concentration and enjoyment where the individual is fully engaged and energized. (Dhiman 2012, 24-33) "When a person is able to organize his or her consciousness so as to experience flow as often as possible, the quality of life is inevitably going to improve". (Csikszentmihalyi 1991, 40) Csikszentmihalyi's research describes the process of flow and how our neurochemistry is profoundly affected by this level of consciousness. Memory based upon previous experiences responds and evaluates the novelty of what is being seen. In our recognition of beauty, we respond to cultural and universal values, which have been part of our cultural and collective consciousness.

Beauty serves as a respite from the intensities of life by providing a respite from the chaos. It is a positive deference reminding us that beauty is innate and accessible. Beauty is restorative in how it helps us return to nature and the rekindle our spirits.

Creative innovation has been inspired by the pursuit of beauty. Throughout human history, art and music have evolved as a means of transcending our human experiences. This has been central to our evolution. During Paleolithic and Neanderthal periods, beauty has been represented through the design and creation of musical instruments, ceramics, and cave paintings. Again the creative process manifested through murals, musical instruments, ceramics, and among the Sumerian, Asian, Greek, and Roman civilizations. The scope of human creative skill spanning over 40,000 years is vast and there is much evidence to support this.

Artists and musicians heal us from the negative aspects of our world by allowing feelings to be expressed and shared. We value the process and the virtuosity involved. As humans we have an innate appreciation for expertise and virtuoso displays in art and music. Virtuosity inspires us and is a catalyst for regarding the world differently. It helps us see what human potential exists and what is possible with perseverance.

From the murals in the Neanderthal caves in Lascaux, France to the experience of being inside the galleries of the Prado Museum in Madrid, we see rich and diverse examples of human mastery. Interestingly, this mastery however, does not always derive from the domain of the able-bodied experts and there is much evidence to show that many individuals challenged by physical and psychological obstacles have demonstrated vast abilities in reaching the heights of their potential. We are humbled by the level of their perseverance and talent often evidenced by the profundity of their work.

While the experience of art and music often has the power of immediacy in making us feel good, the additional experience of making art and music also relates to experiencing pleasure. In this way, the maker and the appreciator can both benefit. It is important to note that the final product can also be valued for its novel or innovative approaches (for example, this is to be seen in the work of John Cage, Andy Warhol, Roy Lichtenstein, Yoyoi Kusama) and that if skillfully rendered inspires awe.

Many studies have shown a correlation between the engagement in the arts and psychological and physical healing. The therapeutic effects are evident in research provided by the medical community. One interesting example that documents music's powerful therapeutic benefits involves a study showing that when music is played through a patient's earphones while undergoing surgery, less anesthesia is required. (Lepage et al. 2001) Another recent example of using music as part of a treatment modality involves research conducted at the Cleveland Clinic in the USA where neurosurgery was conducted on patients suffering from Parkinson's disease. (Carr 2001) The patients remained awake during surgery while wearing earphones listening to soothing music to decrease stress during this complex procedure. Additionally, research published in the Clinical Journal of Pain described a study that assessed the usefulness of music intervention for patients with chronic pain. (Guetin et al. 2012) Eighty-seven patients with back pain, fibromyalgia, inflammatory disease, or neurological disease were included in the study. Forty-four received at least two daily sessions of music listening plus their standard treatment, and then pursued the music intervention at home until day 60 using a multimedia player. At day 60 in the music intervention group, this technique enabled a more significant reduction in pain and significantly reduced anxiety, depression and the use of anti-anxiety medication.

These results confirm the value of music intervention for the management of chronic pain, anxiety and depression. Listening to music can help older adults reduce their levels of depression. Music is a non-invasive, simple, and inexpensive therapeutic method for improving life quality. Another research study was conducted involving 50 older adult depressed patients. (Chan et al. 2012, 776-83) The participants listened to their choice of music for 30 minutes per week for eight weeks. Depression scores were collected once a week for eight weeks. Their levels of depression reduced weekly in the music group, indicating a statistically significant reduction in depression levels due to a cumulative dose effect found over time in the music group compared with the non-music group.

As early as 40,000 years ago in Europe, creative human transformation had begun. Ancient people left evidence of their musical instruments. (Wilford 2012) Flutes made of bird bone and mammoth ivory uncovered in the Danube Valley, Germany which were determined to be 43,000 years old showed how Neanderthals had learned how to capture music through their sensorial perceptions: the auditory. Throughout civilization, musical instruments have been found inside caves, sacred spaces, and at archeological sites. Music has been an important tool for soothing individuals, unifying the tribe, and communicating with the divine. It has been a catalyst for rhythm and dance because music is not just only auditory, but is motor-based and inspires movement.

Moreover, sounds engage us in ways that words do not. Culturally, music and art help us by stimulating imagination and spirituality transforming us into healthier beings. Thus, music is an international language that extinguishes boundaries.

Neanderthal cave paintings discovered in the Nerja Caves in Malaga, Spain were carbon tested. It was determined that the paintings were 42,000 years old. (Mac Erlean 2012) The images were representational and show the intentions of the artists. The artist lived in a world of animals, survival, and hunting. The skills involved in crushing certain rocks to get color pigment and mixing this powder with enough moisture to create a paint paste shows the artistry involved. These paintings reveal how humans visually represented imagery through their sensorial perceptions.

The subjective experience of music connects closely with our emotions and how we feel. The experience of listening has the power to induce feelings of well-being. Music can inspire us to dance, sing, and deeply enjoy what we are hearing. The adage that music can "soothe the savage breast" is well known and scientists have determined that there is a strong relationship between acoustic wave frequencies and emotional states. Due to this, music alleviates anxiety and distracts people from their emotional and physical pain. Biologically, music regulates the brain's limbic system by releasing numerous accompanying neurochemical changes. The elegance of these cadences and changes profoundly affects the individual. It can create an impetus that can distract from negative feelings and ameliorate the influence of past negative memories. Music in fact increases relaxed states of consciousness by decreasing the release of stress hormones. Scientists have

4

determined that people in a relaxed state and a good mood are far more able to concentrate, appreciate beauty, and develop innovative or creative thoughts.

Neuroimaging techniques have provided information as to which parts of the brain are activated during flow and creative engagement. Studies show that, though the emotional experience of listening to music engages many parts of the brain, it is primarily localized in the prefrontal cortex. (Cromie 1997) The prefrontal cortex is intimately involved with the limbic system and our capacity for rational thought (two key elements in perceiving music) provide theoretical evidence for this finding. An immersion in music stimulates the growth of new brain cells in the cerebral cortex. As emotions manifest, feelings manifest within the brain's neurochemistry. Physiological levels are raised in the immune, endocrine, and nervous systems. These areas combine to create a significant psychologically transcendent experience. It is a state of arousal that increases well-being, optimism, and resilience, which are all essential tenants of healing. Research has shown that optimism and feelings of well-being are positively correlated with improved health and morale. (Harvard Medical School, 2008)

Classical musicians and composers provide us with examples of people who consciously attempt to create beauty through the sound of instruments as a way to bring forth a spiritual dimension. For example, the classical cellist Jacqueline du Pres' had healed herself and others through her playing her cello evoking spiritual feelings as a performer and within the response of the audience. Another similar example like du Pres' is the Jewish classical violinist Itzhak Perlman (who had polio). Great composers such as Mozart and Beethoven composed many of their most beautiful works from their sickbeds. In fact, a great deal of the great beauty in music has come out of those afflicted with illness or physical challenges; other examples in this regard include Chopin, Donizetti, Schubert, Schumann, Smetana, and Joplin. (Sartin 2010)

What makes us predisposed to beauty? Are there traits within our personalities that increase a susceptibility to the powers of beauty? As we look more closely into this, we find that there are certain traits and predispositions that increase the transformative experience of beauty in art and music and that several elements are critical to the perception of beauty. (Shapira and Liberman 2009) Persons possessing abilities to engage in fantasy and imagination are more susceptible to beauty. Having a creative imagination increases *hypnotisability*, which is an ability to concentrate deeply, to absorb, and become fascinated. A familiarity with what aesthetics are and experiences of listening to different types of music and seeing a variety of art forms increase artistic sensitivity. (McRae and Costa 1987, 81-90) Moreover, the personality trait of openness to experience, the tendency to suspend judgment, and be curious about the unknown or unfamiliar heightens the ability to be immersed in beauty. Research shows that there is a preponderance of people supportive of the arts that to hold liberal social, religious, and political views. An example of this is found in Pablo Picasso's refusal to exhibit his work or build a museum while Franco was in power.

Having an appreciation of creative mastery and the technical skills required increases the enthusiasm of the observer. There is a deep regard for the tenacity and perseverance involved in producing the final product. Early exposure to the arts has many positive outcomes. For example, musical education begun in early childhood seems to "strengthen a range of auditory skills. Recent studies suggest that these benefits extend all through life, at least for those who continue to be engaged with music." (Klass 2012) Early musical exposure produces a "more robust responses—their brains were better able to pick out essential elements, like pitch. This kind of musical training improves the brain's ability to discern the components of sound-the pitch, the timing and the timbre." Educational curricula and exposure to the arts increases familiarity with these pursuits and develops a base of knowledge to apply to future experiences.

Additionally, individuals predisposed to emotional intelligence, that is, an awareness of feelings of inner emotional states, are able to respond more completely to the subjective experiences of beauty. Art is the need to express ideas from our inner emotions and give us a sense of the divine. It is enhanced by inspiration.

Plato is quoted as saying, "The man who arrives at the doors of artistic creation with none of the madness of the Muses would be convinced that technical ability alone was enough to make an artist... what that man creates by means of reason will pale before the art of inspired beings."

Art is not from our logical constructions but from our inner worlds and from our inner forces. Jackson Pollock exemplifies this process by saying, "The modern artist is living in a mechanical age and we have a mechanical means of representing objects in nature such as the camera and photograph. The modern artist, it seems to me, is working and expressing an inner world—in other words—expressing the energy, the motion and the other inner forces. The modern artist is working with space and time, and expressing his feelings rather than illustrating." (Wright 1950, 139-140)

As such, beautiful art and music furnish us with an imaginative acquaintance with abstraction which stimulates a higher order of perception within the mind's cognitive activities. We share in this tribute that is evidenced by the art, sculpture, and music that has been produced for eons. The German Enlightenment philosopher Kant had believed that our experience of beauty was also revealed in the uniformity of humankind's taste and judgment—a *sensus communis*, meaning a shared human sense. (Dutton 2008, 279-91)

Through what he had called "disinterested contemplation" beauty affects and speaks to us. There are universal values of beauty innate in us, which make us see and value this throughout the history of civilization. The aesthetical pleasure of beauty, which can contain both logical and spiritual dimensions, may also derive from a combination of factors such as logical pleasure, that is, a well-functioning system combined with a 'purposeless' to it and no practical or theoretical gain being involved.

Another important constituent of appreciating the beauty in art and music is our imagination. Imagination furnishes us with the ability for forming new ideas, abstractions, and sensations, which help us to go beyond the ordinariness of the world. It is a catalyst for abstract thinking and novelty. When we use our imaginations, we explore multiple dimensions of thinking; which furthers the understanding that art and music also has multiple meanings. We look for themes and symbolism in how the work is represented as we consider the breadth of the piece and the nuances offered.

"The pursuit of truth and beauty is a sphere of activity in which our lives are permitted to remain children all of our lives." Albert Einstein

Abstract thinking and using the imagination is of benefit to individuals in many ways. This process helps in strategizing creative approaches to problem solving. It invites risk taking and thinking outside of one's mental architecture or "outside the box". This process also allows for a more complex conceptual understanding of the depth of experience. In fact, some early psychiatrists believe that "thinking" is not the only part of abstract knowledge. For example, the Swiss Psychiatrist Carl Jung defined some personality types as having the ability to abstractly feel or sense, in addition to having the ability to think. (Luttrell 2012) Perhaps even more importantly, the artist-musician can stimulate us with opportunities for transcendence (as can be evidenced by the power of listening to extremely beautiful music such as Pergolesi's *Stabat Mater*, Mozart's *Requiem* or Beethoven's *Moonlight Sonata* for example).

Often the creative performer when presenting an opus provides a lens into the core and purpose of the work. This reflects the artist's truth. This fulfills the *telos,* the end of purpose, for the work has been completed and the audience has experienced the work in its entirety.

It is important to also comment on the rich, sensory experiential qualities inherent in art and music. Some might describe this immersion as "dreamy" or feeling a deep spiritual connection and unity. These feelings are induced from the Theta brain waves that are correlated to inspirational feelings, creativity and profound insight. American artist Maxfield Parrish (1870-1966) produced paintings that are known for their dream-like qualities. He used complex glazing techniques combined with layering colors to achieve certain atmospheric landscapes. His figures are often positioned against vivid, skies that reflect great beauty. His illumination of the American landscape provides it with an otherworldly dimension. One example of this is to be found in his painting "The Lute Players", where he invites the viewer into the dream state to imagine the ethereal music being played by the muses.

A parallel process to this also occurs when immersing oneself in music. Music activates the associated with dream states. In this way, music deepens us as it invites us to experience deeper sensations.

By creating an immersive 'experience' in beautiful art and music our neurochemistry experiences rapid perceptual changes, increasing our self-awareness and sensory perceptions. The cascade of neurochemicals triggers a decrease in stress hormones within us. The brain's opioid system, which blocks pain, slows breathing, and creates a sense of well-being.

Sometimes, when we are put in this immersive state, we experience being inside the music, or inside the art while correspondingly being aware that we are also on the outside as spectators. When we visually perceive beauty, information from the retinal cells in our eyes travels to our visual cortex in the brain's occipital lobe. (Brown and Gao 2011) Imagery then travels to brain centers with specific cells for orientation to the lines, shapes, and colors we perceive. The visual image travels to the temporal lobe where a comparative analysis occurs. It is a process that facilitates analysis and helps us value and appreciate what we are experiencing.

When the brain hears music, a series a physiological sequence occurs. (Cromie 1997) Music modulates the brain's limbic system by triggering numerous accompanying neurochemical effects. The inner ear contains a spiral sheet that the sounds of music pluck like guitar strings. The plucking triggers the firing of synapses that make up the hearing parts of the brain. The auditory cortex, above the ears, generates the conscious experience of music. Different patterns of firing excite other ensembles of cells and these associate the sounds of music with feelings and thoughts. This opens our minds to new links, possibilities, deepening our knowledge of ourselves and others and our relation to human existence and the universe.

Often immersion in nature is a catalyst in increasing our sense of beauty. It intensifies feelings already existing in us that are partially reflected in the epiphanies experienced when we see the peaks of a mountain range enveloped by clouds, a vivid sunset reflecting upon the water, or a full moon encircled by orbs in a night sky. We behold these experiences and receive pleasure from them. Many artists have been inspired by nature and this is often the genesis of their art. Examples can be seen in the works of the English Romantic artists of the nineteenth century. Many of Samuel Palmer's paintings (1805-1881), have been said to disclose the artist's rich inner life and in them, one sees that they unveil his awareness that there is something of a "divine secret of art" within the soul of the perceiver who overhears the expression of nature communicating its unlimited mysteries. (Blayney-Brown 2001, 24)

'Beauty' thus gives us the meaning of life. It lifts us up to higher spiritual and moral planes. It is therefore a value synonymous with creativity that never stops being as important as goodness and truth against soulnessness and self-centeredness in a modern world of randomness and egocentricity. In this way, the beauty in music and art has an ethereal dimension, which both have the potential to deepen our personal values and greatly enrich our understanding of the world.

References

Blayney-Brown, David. 2001. Romanticism. London: Phaidon Press.

Brown, Stephen and Xiaging Gao, 2011. "Neuroscience of Beauty." Scientific American, September 27. http://www.scientificamerican.com/article.cfm?id=the-neuroscience-of-beauty <accessed 9/10/12>

Carr, Coeli. 2009. "Using Music to Ease Patient Stress During Surgery." *Time Magazine*, October 13. http://www.time.com/time/health/article/0,8599,1929994,00.html <accessed 9/12/12>

Chan, Moon Fai, Yang Wong Zi, Hideaki Onishi and Naidu Vellasamy Thayala 2012. "Effects of Music on Depression in Older People: A Randomised Controlled Trial. *Journal of Clinical Nursing*. 21 (5-6): 776-83.

Cromie, William J. 1997. "How Your Brain Listen to Music." *Harvard University Gazette*, November 13. http://www.news.harvard.edu/gazette/1997/11.13/HowYourBrainLis.html <accessed 9/12/12>

Csikszentmihalyi, Mihaly. 1991. Flow: The Psychology of Optimal Experience. New York: Harper Collins.

Dhiman, Satinder 2012. "Mindfullness and the Art of Living Creatively." Journal of Social Change 4: 24-33.

Dutton, Denis. 2008. "Aesthetic Universals." In The Routledge Companion to Aesthetics, edited by Berys Gaut and Dominic McIver Lopes, 279-291. Oxford, England: Routledge.

Guetin, Stephane, Patrick, Siou, Didier Kong et al. "The Effects of Music Intervention in the Management of Chronic Pain: A Single-Blind, Randomized, Controlled Trial". *Clinical Journal of Pain*. 28 (4): 329-37.

Harvard Medical School. 2008. "Why Optimists Enjoy Better Health." *Harvard Medical Publication*, May. http://www.health.harvard.edu/press_releases/why-optimists-enjoy-better-health <accessed 9/11/12>

Interview by William Wright, Summer 1950 as quoted in Abstract Expressionism: Creators and Critics, edited by Clifford Ross, New York: Abrahams Publishers, 1990, 139-140.

Klass, Perry. 2012. "Brain Waves Stay Tuned to Early Lessons." *New York Times*, September 11. http://well.blogs.nytimes.com/2012/09/10/early-music-lessons-have-longtime-benefits/ <accessed 9/11/12>

Klass, Perry. 2012. "Brain Waves Stay Tuned to Early Lessons." *New York Times*, September 11. http://well.blogs.nytimes.com/2012/09/10/early-music-lessons-have-longtime-benefits/ <accessed 9/11/12>

Lepage, Caroline, Pierre Drolet, M. Gerard et al. "The Effect of Music on the

Neuralhormonal Stress Response to Surgery under general Anesthesia. Maisonneuve-Rosemont Hospital and University of Montreal, Montreal, Quebec, Canada, 2001. 93: 912–16.

Luttrell, Andy. 2009. "The Personality Theory of Carl Jung." *Suite 101*, November 16. http://suite101.com/article/the-personality-theory-of-carl-jung-a170440 <accessed 9/12/12>

Mac Erlean, Fergal, 2012. "First Neanderthal Cave Paintings Discovered in Spain." *New Scientist*, February 12. http://www.newscientist.com/article/dn21458-first-neanderthal-cave-paintings-discovered-in-spain. Life html <accessed 9/12/12>

Martin, Agnes and Dieter Schwarz "Writings"book of writings published to accompany the exhibition, "Agnes Martin: Paintings and Works on Paper, 1960-1989, Kunstmuseum Winterthur, Switzerland, January 1992.

McCrae, Robert R. and Paul T. Costa. 1987. "Validation of the Five factor Model of Personality Across Instruments and Observers", *Journal of Personality and Social Psychology*, 52 (1): 81-90.

Oren, Shapira and Nira Liberman. 2009. "An Easy Way to Increase Creativity." *Scientific American*, July 21. http://www.scientificamerican.com/article.cfm?id=an-easy-way-to-increase-c <accessed 9/11/12>

Sartin, Jeffrey S. 2010. "Contagious Diseases Rhythm: Infectious Diseases of 20th Century Musicians." *Clinical Medicine and Research*, July 1. http://www.clinmedres.org/content/8/2/106.full <accessed 9/9/12>

Wilford, John Noble. 2012. "Flute's Revised Age Dates the Sound of Music Earlier." *N.Y. Times*, May 29. http://www.nytimes.com/2012/05/29/science/oldest-musical-instruments-are-even-older-than-first-thought.html?_r=0 <accessed 9/12/12>

YOUR KNOWLEDGE HAS VALUE

- We will publish your bachelor's and
  master's thesis, essays and papers

- Your own eBook and book -
  sold worldwide in all relevant shops

- Earn money with each sale

Upload your text at www.GRIN.com
and publish for free